ONCE UPON A DREAM

Dreams Of Wonder

Edited By Lynsey Evans

First published in Great Britain in 2024 by:

Young Writers
Remus House
Coltsfoot Drive
Peterborough
PE2 9BF
Telephone: 01733 890066
Website: www.youngwriters.co.uk

All Rights Reserved
Book Design by Ashley Janson
© Copyright Contributors 2024
Softback ISBN 978-1-83565-867-3
Printed and bound in the UK by BookPrintingUK
Website: www.bookprintinguk.com
YB0608B

FOREWORD

Welcome Reader, to a world of dreams.

For Young Writers' latest competition, we asked our writers to dig deep into their imagination and create a poem that paints a picture of what they dream of, whether it's a make-believe world full of wonder or their aspirations for the future.

The result is this collection of fantastic poetic verse that covers a whole host of different topics. Let your mind fly away with the fairies to explore the sweet joy of candy lands, join in with a game of fantasy football, or you may even catch a glimpse of a unicorn or another mythical creature. Beware though, because even dreamland has dark corners, so you may turn a page and walk into a nightmare!

Whereas the majority of our writers chose to stick to a free verse style, others gave themselves the challenge of other techniques such as acrostics and rhyming couplets. We also gave the writers the option to compose their ideas in a story, so watch out for those narrative pieces too!

Each piece in this collection shows the writers' dedication and imagination – we truly believe that seeing their work in print gives them a well-deserved boost of pride, and inspires them to keep writing, so we hope to see more of their work in the future!

CONTENTS

Avonmouth C of E (VC) Primary School, Avonmouth

Bella-Rose Sterry (10)	1
Titus Kruszynski (10)	2
Bruno Kruszynski (10)	4
Elsie McGregor (10)	5
Mya Kendall (10)	6
Sandra Piela (10)	8
Kaycie-Mae Green (10)	9
Mason Perry (9)	10
Charles Adeniran (10)	11
Laci Summers (9)	12
Sonny-Bleu Tyler (10)	13
Daniel Kulpa Basovs (10)	14
Jakub Gientka (10)	15
Tiano Forrest (10)	16
Sevde Agac (10)	17
Jamaine Dixon (10)	18
Alma Vasilache (10)	19
Summer Trembath (9)	20

Brookfields Primary School, Hockley

Sophia Omoniyi (10)	22
Hilary Tiago (11)	24
Maryam Surak (10)	26
Aliya (10)	28
Alma Alaawaj (10)	30
Sulayman Ledgister (9)	32
Mardiyah Bilal-Mohammed (11)	34
Manvitha Metukuru (11)	35
Zuriel Aleje (9)	36
Mirabel Egbujor Nmesoma (9)	37
Abdulazeez Awodeko (10)	38

La'kai Thomas (9)	39
Ahwan Adil (10)	40
Kishan Metukuru (9)	41
Richie Obi (10)	42
Ameelah Plummer	43
Robina Katawazai (8)	44
Hafsa Rahat (9)	45
Iasmin Ricci (9)	46
Aliya Yusuf (8)	47
David Omosigho (9)	48
Munachi Asidanya (9)	49
Fatoumatta Ceesay (9)	50
Zainab Khizar (10)	51
Ahlam Alsasi (9)	52
Omar Osman (9)	53
Aarush Naresh Kitey (9)	54
Taha Yagoub (9)	55

Godmanchester Community Academy, Godmanchester

Lola Wilson (10)	56
Theo Oxenbould (10)	57
Arthur Jupe (10)	58

Goffs Oak Primary School, Goffs Oak

Ellie Peone (7)	59
Casper White (8)	60
Alessia McDonald (7)	62
Sophie Georgou (8)	64
Evangeline Christofi (8)	65
Jessica Gray (8)	66
Despina Chanoglou (8)	68
Mehmet A (8)	70

Stefan Vourloumic (8)	71
Bentley Barclay (8)	72
Sienna Demetriou (8)	73
Sylvie Brandy (8)	74
Chloe C (8)	75
Grace Steel (8)	76
Lara Djelil (8)	77
Alessia Antoniou (8)	78
Ryan Henry-Macklin (8)	79
Emre Kargi (8)	80
Sienna Tse (8)	81
Maria Georgiades (8)	82
Roman Winter (8)	83
Sophia Georgiades (8)	84

Hampton Hill Junior School, Hampton Hill

Qasim Ali (8)	85
Federico Orlando (10)	86
Ammar Ali (10)	88
Jesse Turner (9)	89
Jacob Hollis (10)	90
Isabella Richardson (8)	91
Meg Porteous (9)	92
Eleanor Porteous (9)	93
Ahmed Abani (9)	94
Dia Tandon (8)	95

Kennall Vale School, Truro

Henry Hall (9)	96
Freya TS (9)	99
Edan Fyffe (9)	100
Ayla P (9)	102
Jude (9)	104
Beau Main (9)	105
Aubrey French (9)	106
Ayla R (10)	108
Ailla Mulhern (9)	109
Lottie W (9)	110
Elliot S (8)	112
Oriole L (10)	113
Hugo Z (9)	114

Jamie T (9)	115
Ella Thompson (9)	116
Layla Young (10)	117
Isolde R (9)	118
Eli E (10)	119
Elijah Wickes (9)	120
Rowan P	121
Lyra C (9)	122
Jake M (9)	123
Phoebe Young (10)	124
Joby S (9)	125
Travis (9)	126
Hugo Meagor (9)	127
Arthur R (9)	128

Rokeby Primary School, Rugby

Yashnoor Nahar (10)	129
Luna Overton (10)	130
Victoria Szymala (8)	131
Connie Barnes (10)	132
Muqeet Shaik (10)	133
Jackson Jewers (9)	134
Judaea Clarke (8)	135
Kushi Sachin (8)	136
James Taylor-Gittins (9)	137
Gerald Kanini (9)	138
Sienna Bilby (8)	139
Jacob King (9)	140
Kabinin Ibrahim (10)	141
Jordyn Crouch (8)	142
Zawe Salahadin (8)	143
Tyanna Beckford (7)	144
Henry Gravell (8)	145
Marlon Walder (8)	146
Edy Soare (9)	147
Charlie Platt (7)	148
Oliver O'Donnell (8)	149
Isabel Stanhope (8)	150

Springbank Academy, Eastwood

Abigail Maisey (9)	151

St Wilfrid's Catholic Primary School, Angmering

Jemima Kavhu (10)	152
Caitlan Hayler (10)	154
Amelia Dudley (9)	156
Florrie Bloomer (9)	157

The Discovery School, West Malling

Kyan Enver (8)	158
Olivia Read (8)	160
Ella Wigg (8)	161
Tess Oakley (8)	162
Bella Winzar (8)	163
Camille Prescott (7)	164
Olivia Gorman (8)	165
Arhaan Pamnani (8)	166
Eden Lawson (8)	167
Max O'Brien (8)	168
Rayaan Gul (8)	169
Lauren Lee (7)	170
Andreas Hussain (7)	171
Lucy Newton (8)	172
Monique Bailey (7)	173
Winston Wahlers (7)	174
Flossie Wheatley (8)	175

THE CREATIVE WRITING

The Nightmare Loop

N othing has prepared me for this terrifying cemetery,
I look around, there's a person in front of me,
G laring at him he walks towards me,
H ow did I get here? I don't belong here with him,
T he man started to run at me I ran as fast as I could,
M aybe I was overreacting he was only a black figure,
A disaster happened, I fell over, oh no he saw me!
R ight when I got up he captured me,
E erie eyes glowed when I shut mine in fright,
S uddenly, I broke free when I realised I was in a loop.

N othing has prepared me for this cemetery,
I look around, a person is there,
G laring at him he takes a step near me,
H ow did he know I was here with him?
T he sky suddenly turned black with stars,
M oving around the bushes rattled weirdly,
A snake rattled his tail and the man moved,
R ight when I moved a stick snapped,
E ventually, I woke up in a fright.

Bella-Rose Sterry (10)
Avonmouth C of E (VC) Primary School, Avonmouth

Jinxed: Retold

Out in the main estuary,
Ten Cents and Sunshine found a tug astray.
His name was Boomer, very jinxed, he was.
He had his own laws.
He moaned, "Go away,"
But the switchers brought him anyway.
Then they gave him coal,
But smoke bellowed as Captain Star yelled,
"Pull him out!"
But Boomer was as happy on a stroll.
Soon, he was brought near Lucky's Yard,
But Boomer had some shards.
Then, with a little clink, he soon started to slowly sink!
They'd have to bring floating cranes, as strong as seven planes.
First, Mighty Mo and Scuttlebutt Pete, as both helped to complete.
Soon, Sunshine brought Little Ditcher,
His work was done for the small switcher.
Then the cranes lifted Boomer up,
But the ropes were as slippy as ketchup.
Mighty Mo had a tricky time.
As Boomer was heavy, like a box of grime.

OJ and Big Mac brought a marker light,
But soon became out of sight.
Ten Cents hooted,
As the way they went was clearer than suited.
But then, it happened, crashing, banging,
Clashing, smashing, splashing,
The incident was *terrible!*
Then Boomer helped the Z-Stacks,
To help contracts keep on their own tracks.
But then a massive explosion occurred,
Yet Boomer just happily slurred.
Later it was decided, Boomer would pull a schooner,
As jinxes would disappear sooner.
But alas, it caught on fire;
A lightning bolt was its desire!
After that Captain Starr ordered that Boomer would never be a tug again,
He thought he was an unlucky hen.
But as Ten Cents found Boomer as a houseboat,
He was happy as he was afloat.
Soon Ten Cents and Sunshine went away
But Boomer in his new home, was to stay.

Titus Kruszynski (10)
Avonmouth C of E (VC) Primary School, Avonmouth

Flying

Flying with Superman is super fun,
Over the clouds and up above,
Flying over trees as I'm pleased,
Having fun with the doves,
Carrying a jar full of dreams, sending them into homes to make them pleased,
Flying chickens with us, wearing ribbons above us,
Catching butterflies as we fly,
As the doves head us past we fly really fast,
Flowers blooming really high, while we're in the sky,
As a plane passed us quickly, some rain drizzled us slick,
As gods watch us from above, the sun shines on and on,
As I slept in my bed, my cat crept under my chair.

Bruno Kruszynski (10)
Avonmouth C of E (VC) Primary School, Avonmouth

Never-Ending Mummies

In the night sky, far, far away,
Floats a candy kingdom,
That's not there during the day.
Trees made out of lollipops,
The road made of sugar,
Driving on the sugary roads,
Making my upper half shiver.
Up ahead, appear sudden mummies,
Colours of the rainbow, walking like dummies.
Chased away, I come across a shed,
Mummies grumbling behind me,
I'll hide in there instead.
I step into the shed,
To find my mum sat down,
Staring straight ahead, not looking around.
I sit on her lap, as I look straight forward,
The mummies come closer and closer.
All of a sudden, we're cornered.
Suddenly, I open my eyes
To my surprise, I'm in my warm bed,
Safe and sound,
No mummies lurking around.

Elsie McGregor (10)
Avonmouth C of E (VC) Primary School, Avonmouth

Dream Big

I close my eyes every night,
With eyes shut closed,
Going into a dream, mind turning back and forth.
Bam! There is a dream so wide,
Full of mystery.
Where could they take you?
Nobody knows.

I just find myself standing there,
Dream cat right in front of me,
Staring right at it.
Now happy tears run down my warm face,
Never wanting this to end,
Never ever,
Not even once in a million years,
Hoping that it'll stay forever.

Morning is getting new,
Now decorating everything.
Eyes starting to wake.
"Why right now?" I shout out loud.
"Why can't I stay?
Why, why, why?"

Dream starting to fade away,
It is like a loop,
Happening all over again.

All I see now is darkness,
Then a burst of light.
"It's over," I say.

Mya Kendall (10)
Avonmouth C of E (VC) Primary School, Avonmouth

Once Upon A Dream

Once upon a dream,
I saw a monkey spinning like a ballerina,
It was extreme,
I saw a hippo in a cowboy hat,
And then out of the hat leapt out a cat,
I smelt steam coming from my right,
I crept over in a fright,
Just to see a cow cooking pasta,
What a sight!

Once upon a dream,
I saw chickens with sunglasses,
And hairy moustaches,
Drinking orange juice from wine glasses,
I saw a rhino spraying whipped cream,
On his head in bed,
I saw a snake holding a rake,
Trying to catch fish from a lake,

Well that wasn't a dream to expect,
But it's not the end yet.

Sandra Piela (10)
Avonmouth C of E (VC) Primary School, Avonmouth

Lovely Dreams

L ovely fairies came across my eyes
O range unicorns fly through the skies
V ery cute animals fluffy and small
E legant butterfly wings like wool
L onely trees swaying with glee
Y ummy gummy bears danced in front of me.

D ogs are so cute running around chasing butterflies
R ude reindeer came up to me shaking their tails being funny
E vil eagles swooped down getting groovy
A liens friendly came down and let me explore their ship
M y heart singing with pure joy
S uddenly I woke up in my bed wishing this dream wouldn't end!

Kaycie-Mae Green (10)
Avonmouth C of E (VC) Primary School, Avonmouth

Untitled

At home I was in my bed. My dog woke me up and I heard a big bang. I opened my door and went down the stairs. I didn't see anything except the living room light. I turned it off and got my water and went upstairs. I jumped back in my bed and went to sleep. I was in an abandoned house and I heard a creepy laugh. Then I found a gun on the floor and a clown jumped out of nowhere. My dog wanted to bite the clown. Luckily he was on the leash. He had smoke coming out of his nose. Then he did a random noise, then loads of clowns came over. I shot one, but he did not die because he had a bulletproof vest on. When I woke up I was in my bed.

Mason Perry (9)
Avonmouth C of E (VC) Primary School, Avonmouth

Nightmare

In my dream, I was in my house but I saw a hole. I went in and I saw some creepy clowns chasing me. Then I fell on the ground and I saw a mystery door. I went in and I saw skeletons crawling like spiders but the clowns were still chasing me. There was an exit but it was closing. I ran quickly and I finally went in but the ground was open. I fell in and I saw my sister and she was scared. I noticed that it was not my house so I found a secret door and went in. Monsters were chasing us but my sister was tired and she was asleep. I carried her and I saw another exit and we went in. The hole closed and I saw my mum and dad again.

Charles Adeniran (10)
Avonmouth C of E (VC) Primary School, Avonmouth

Nightmare

At home where I lay, I have a scary nightmare.
Then I hear noises from the sink and below.
I check, I look in the sink, I see nothing more.
Then I see something standing.
I go over on my own, I see it's a clown.
I run away, shouting for my mum.
I feel really dizzy and everything's spinning.
Hopefully this is a joke, all I see is smoke.
Then I turn myself around and see the clown.
He opens his eyes and starts to run after me.
When I lose the scary clown, my mum and sister run down.
They look up and down the house, seeing no signs of any clowns.

Laci Summers (9)
Avonmouth C of E (VC) Primary School, Avonmouth

Fortnite With My Duo (Haydn)

Warm-up, two versus two piece control.
Playing piece control to warm up.
Pump snipe every round around and around.
Ten to five, it was an easy win.
Rematch after rematch, win after win, easier and easier.
It was so easy, we left because they rage quit.
Ranked game.
We land and kill the duo but the duo is all I see.
We move to Lavish Lair, a killing spree we share.
We move to Grimgate as the car shakes as far as can be
As well as can be, Grimgate we see.
As we enter Cerberus admits defeat.
Then we accept the win.

Sonny-Bleu Tyler (10)
Avonmouth C of E (VC) Primary School, Avonmouth

The Scary Night Before Disaster

N othing can help me in this strange dream.
I have to hide somewhere so secretive.
G oing far I find a weird alley.
H iding inside I feel so uneasy.
T ime keeps ticking it is blood-chilling.
M any seconds later I woke up spooked.
A fter some time I realised I was tired.
R ealising that, I sat on the window.
E ventually something broke through the door.
S uddenly I wake up and I'm safe.

Daniel Kulpa Basovs (10)
Avonmouth C of E (VC) Primary School, Avonmouth

Nightmare

N ight-time has come, it's dark and scary,
I look out my window, I see something hairy,
G ive me some peace, I really need it now,
H ow did someone get in? I hear a loud howl,
T hings disappear, also I feel fear,
M aybe something has come, I can hear,
A lso, why are there white lights flickering?
R ight, why is there a long snake slithering?
E arly in the morning, I've woken up now.

Jakub Gientka (10)
Avonmouth C of E (VC) Primary School, Avonmouth

Nightmares

N obody can be prepared for what I see.
I take a step around the strange land.
G reat monsters move around, they look like a band.
H ow did I get here, how can I get out?
T here was a shadow all alone moving.
M y eyes got to see it, my worst fear.
A gigantic, terrifying dragon, it got near.
R unning and flying towards me.
E yes as big as a bus, as it hits me, I fall out of my bed.

Tiano Forrest (10)
Avonmouth C of E (VC) Primary School, Avonmouth

My Nightmare

In my nightmare tonight,
I heard a girl in the
Basement crying, loud like
She was going to die.

In my nightmare tonight,
At night, on a Wednesday
The girl in the basement
Was making tapping noises.

When I woke up, I was
On the floor, then I said,
"It was a nightmare I guess."
But my nightmare never stopped.

Sevde Agac (10)
Avonmouth C of E (VC) Primary School, Avonmouth

My Scary Nightmare

Stepping through the door, this doesn't look like my floor
Something taunting, I think this place is haunted
I look at the ceiling, I see a goblin eating
I open a bunker, this looks abandoned
I'm coming out of the bunker, then I hear lots of thunder
Am I done yet? Why can I not have fun again?
I open a door, oh look, it's my dorm.

Jamaine Dixon (10)
Avonmouth C of E (VC) Primary School, Avonmouth

My Nightmare

In between 3am or 3:30am
I heard something moving in my house
I went to see it, I saw my book had moved to another place
And my ball was moved after I saw my pen move
I woke up, I was safe in bed.

Alma Vasilache (10)
Avonmouth C of E (VC) Primary School, Avonmouth

Buffet

In my dreams
I saw loads of
Food containing
Sausages
Eggs
Hash browns
And beans
As that happened
My belly filled
With glee.

As we sat
At our table
A waiter came
His name was
Dale
He came
And I ordered
Lots of food
After that
I was in
A mood

With a full
Stomach and
Wobbled back
To the car.

Summer Trembath (9)
Avonmouth C of E (VC) Primary School, Avonmouth

Once Upon A Dream

Have you ever heard this story?
It might get sappy, maybe gory
I warn you all is not as it seems
But it started with once upon a dream

A place where imagination is sold
A realm with wishes untold
Now let's go deeper with a key
And unlock the magical block of dreams

So, this is what happens and unfolds
Lots of riches, with lots of gold
Superheroes flying up high
The brightest star in the night jewelled sky

We all have our aspirations
Not as plenty as our imaginations
Some of us are very keen
But there's a rule a dream must always remain unseen

Okay, okay listen closely, this is about to get very scary,
So, you must be brave most of all, cautious and wary
This is not going to be a walk in the park
Warning, the dreamland will get very dark

You might be asking me what is going on well
Well some people might be able to tell all
But in the book, it clearly states
A dream and a nightmare were once best mates
Have you ever heard this story?

The nightmare was then cast away
A land none can stay
Every once and then it breaks the spell
And makes Dreamland a living hell

I could now smell some kitchen steam
I awoke from my slumber, my once-upon-a-dream
Oh, look we are at the end of the chapter
I guess we got our happily ever after
Fine I'll be nice
Under one price.

Sophia Omoniyi (10)
Brookfields Primary School, Hockley

The Journey Of Albort: From The Forest To The Football Field

In the enchanted woods, where the wild bears dwell,
A tale of an adventure I'm eager to tell.
A bear with a dream, to Germany he'll roam,
For the Euros await, a footballer's home.

Through lush green valleys and mountains so towering,
He embarks on a journey, reaching for the sky.
With each pawstep forward, determination in his eyes,
He is fuelled by passion, ready to mesmerise.

In Germany's embrace, he finds his new stage,
Where football is celebrated, with boundless rage.
On the grand football pitch, he takes his rightful place,
A bear among players, showcasing his grace.

With thunderous steps, he charges through the field,
His strength and agility a powerful shield.
The crowd roars with excitement, as he scores a hat-trick,
A bear in the Euros, a story to be told.

His presence commands attention, a force to be reckoned,
In the hearts of fans, his legend is beckoned.
With every match, his game continues to rise,
A bear with a mission, reaching for the skies.

So let us cheer for the bear, as he takes the stage,
In Germany's embrace, he's found his football stage.
With passion and skill, he'll conquer the game,
A bear in the Euros, forever his name.

Hilary Tiago (11)
Brookfields Primary School, Hockley

Dear Black Girl

Dear Black Girl,
Embrace the beauty that lies within,
Let your melanin shine; let it begin,
Your skin, like ebony, holds a story untold,
A tale of strength, resilience and pure gold!

Don't hide in the shadows; let your voice be heard,
God created you with love and admiration; you are too beautiful, and listen to my word,
Stand tall, let your confidence soar,
For your presence alone is a sight to adore.

Dear Black Girl,
Let your hair be a crown, a symbol of pride,
Embrace its texture and its volume; let it glide,
From coils to curls, from kinks to waves,
Your hair is a masterpiece, a crown that truly amazes.

Rock your Afro; let it stand tall and free,
Or twist it up into beautiful braids; let it be,
Experiment with styles, express yourself with flair,
For your hair is a canvas, a work of art to wear.

So, dear Black Girl,
Embrace your heritage and grace,
For you are a masterpiece, a work of art in this space,
Let your hair shine bright,
Embrace its magic and its might,
Don't listen to the others who tell you to hide,
For they are just jealous inside.

Maryam Surak (10)
Brookfields Primary School, Hockley

The Little Boy

Far, far away, when the little boy grew up
He was so scared to hold a cup
Because it was made out of glass
In the summer, he liked to play in the grass.

He went to Brookfields Primary School
The next day, he was standing on a stool
His favourite colour was purple
His favourite shape was a circle.

He loved to comb his hair
He loved to take care
The next day, he cried
Because he wanted to go outside.

He wanted to go for a swim
But his dad had to go to the gym
He loved making jokes
He liked drinking Coke.

His hobby was eating chocolate bars
At night, he saw the stars
He looked through the window
And he saw a rainbow.

Outside, he saw a dog
But the air was full of fog
He talked to his mum
He was chewing gum.

His name was Maxi
He waited for a taxi
He loved running around the park
He was scared of the sharks.

He bought a new cat
Which was very fat
Which he doesn't like
He plays with his new bike.

Aliya (10)
Brookfields Primary School, Hockley

Enchanted Forest

It all started that day on a peaceful night
When I was tired and exhausted from school.
I dreamed this magical enchanted dream
Where birds were flying and making a tune,
In a forest where the moonlight weaved through the branches,
Dense with shining leaves, dwelled creatures with eyes like glass.
Owl-fox hybrids in shadows passed their feathers
And whispered, tails like fire,
Silent as night, yet hearts of choir.
All of a sudden, I heard a whisper.
I came closer to hearing the sound,
Then I felt something that came near me in twilight's hush.
They gathered around where secrets were kept
And legends were told.
A circle formed, the conversation to share their tales
Beneath the light in all of haste,
I heard a sound never felt, like a human or a storm.
They started shouting, "Come out,"
All I could do was shout and run.

They started following me and started yelling at me to come back.
After I got tired and couldn't take a single breath.

Alma Alaawaj (10)
Brookfields Primary School, Hockley

The Trio Of Travellers

In my dreams, every night,
I travel below the sky that is so bright,
I look all around me, and all I see are trees,
And all I can hear are buzzing bees,
I gather my group,
Then take them out for soup,
We are travelling all day long,
And while we travel, we sing a song,
Every time we enter a village,
There's always someone looking to pillage,
But we always stop it,
And when we do, we throw them into the dungeon pit!
Sometimes we stop for family and friends time,
A chance to share out sweet limes.

T ime goes by in my dreams every night
R unning away because my fears are so bright
A dventures await but
V illains are awake
E agerly, waiting like a pauper
L uring them in to perform the slaughter
L aying low, so as not to be spotted
I ntensely waiting with a throbbing carotid
N othing has prepared me for this strange place I see
G lancing left and right, all I see are trees.

Sulayman Ledgister (9)
Brookfields Primary School, Hockley

The Pride Of A Lion

Eyes like royal blue, serene like serene sea
When provoked triggered by a violent breeze
His face as sensitive as tears on silk
His voice calm like cosy mother's milk
His nose noble nobility sparkling through
His eyebrows demonstrative when sharply pointed at you
His back strict straight shoulders show pride
His mane rowdy and shows his wild side
In his voice he is quiet, silent as time
But his face to the world he faces with pride
His hands he uses to expect what's within
But they weave his magic don't tolerate sin
His feet lead with purpose issue a threat
If you mess with a lion don't value your head
His heart shows a softness if you can get through
Only with honesty shrewdness and virtue
An admirable man his inside is golden
But never expect that his will will be broken
You may want to be you, may want mystique
But you'll never attain what makes him unique.

Mardiyah Bilal-Mohammed (11)
Brookfields Primary School, Hockley

Echoes Of Eternity

One night, I fell into a deep sleep,
And found myself in a world so mystical and sweet.
I floated on soft, fluffy clouds so serene,
In a magical place unlike anything I'd seen.

All around me were wondrous sights,
Luminous lights shining in the sky so bright.
Tall mountains rose up, reaching so high,
While whispers drifted by, making me want to go and try.

To explore this realm of magic and wonder,
I was totally amazed, filled with awe down under,
At all the amazing things my eyes could see,
Wishing I could stay in this dream world, happy and free.

I'm reluctantly pulled back, my senses still captivated,
The memory of its timeless, ancient quality lingers.
I will forever seek to recapture the deep feeling of peace,
That washed over me in that sublime, fantastical realm.

Manvitha Metukuru (11)
Brookfields Primary School, Hockley

In My Dreams Every Night

In my dreams every night, people ask for autographs,
Walking on the red carpet, while phones get photos of me.
While walking with my friends, we get selfies like we are celebrities, or actors, or singers.

People are scattered in the concert while I am singing.
My friends are at the back, dancing on the stage like stage dancers.
After the concert, I get in the car like a singer that had an amazing day.

Back in the studio, thinking about which movie would be great for the cinemas.
It feels like I am an actor, or singer, or a celebrity.
And I feel like it is in real life.

But while I'm in the studio, I plan ideas for my new song.
But I'm also thinking of a singing or acting role.
I could be in a movie.

Zuriel Aleje (9)
Brookfields Primary School, Hockley

Magical Creatures

In a mysterious and magical land,
I see fairies blowing trumpets and space astronauts calling my name (echoing).
Glancing at first sight, seeing flying dancers and footballers.
Also in Heaven, whispering bedtime stories and songs.
Famous angels and wizards doing superpowers,
Dragons breathing fire from their mouths.
Pirates in their ships spying with telescopes.
In a cave getting lost all by myself,
The royal family coming to save me.
Monsters and sea octopuses fighting for food in the water.
Clowns jump-scaring people
And unicorns using their horns to put magical spells.
I went back to reality and I look forward to having another great imagination in a magical world, such as an adventure.
What a wonderful dream!

Mirabel Egbujor Nmesoma (9)
Brookfields Primary School, Hockley

The Footballer With Superpower

In my dreams sometimes I think, what would it be like if a footballer had superpowers? So I am writing this because of my dream.

Once upon a dream, there was a haunted stadium with special footballers who had superpowers. One was the favourite called Max. He was so good that he single-handedly destroyed every team with his powers and skills. He was so good that it was nearly impossible to beat him. Other teams were scared to go against him. He was also captain. Everyone loved him.

I wish I could see him but I'm from a different planet called Jupiter. The largest planet of every single one of the other planets. Next year I might just be able to see him in the moonlight...

Abdulazeez Awodeko (10)
Brookfields Primary School, Hockley

The Boy Who Could Fly

Once upon a time, a boy named La'kai was in his room; his window was open, and then lightning struck him and some chemicals.

The next morning, he woke up and got dressed for school until he tripped over a bottle and fell out the window. He got scared, but then he was floating. He was wondering how he was floating until he remembered yesterday!

He went to school walking, but after school, he started going to an abandoned place to learn how to control his new powers until he saw on the news that there was a villain.

He went to get a costume, then went to fight the villain, and it was a long fight until he did a super punch. The city was saved, and he became a superhero.

La'kai Thomas (9)
Brookfields Primary School, Hockley

Books Can Get You Anywhere

Books are really fun to read
Some about dragging horses with a lead
Others are about wizards and fantasy
That you can read on the canopy

Some books make you feel calm
Others feel like you're in a swarm
As you close your head into a book
You're dancing with the world's kindest cook

You walk and find a mysterious hole
And in it there's a bright white pole
Which is guarded with a venomous snake
And makes you have a really bad headache

Some books can leave you mind-blown
Like if you go into the unknown
Books can go really far
And can also go quite bizarre.

Ahwan Adil (10)
Brookfields Primary School, Hockley

Unknown Monster

In the shadowed depths where moonlight flees,
There stirs something amidst the trees.
Its breath a whisper, cold and stark,
Echoes softly through the dark.
Eyes like coal of smouldered night,
Gleam with hunger, fierce and bright.
Claws that scrape the earth below,
Leave trails of fear where shadows grow.
It slinks through the mist of ancient lore,
A creature none have seen before.
A howl, a cry, a mournful wail,
Tells where the others fail.
For in the dark, the monster bides,
In shadow cloaks, it's safely hidden.
Beware the whisper on the breeze
Of the unknown beast that no one sees.

Kishan Metukuru (9)
Brookfields Primary School, Hockley

Mysterious Powers

In a mysterious park,
I found a potion that was really dark,
If I drank it I might turn pale,
But what if all of this was a tale?
After I finished devouring it,
It gave me superpowers that were lit,
It was my destiny to find what they can be,
Suddenly, I tripped and bumped my knee,
I was surprised I didn't feel any pain,
Or even make a simple complaint,
I figured out I can't get hurt,
So I decided what to do first,
Realising I have infinite health,
All of a sudden I got freeze breath,
But all I wanted was super flight,
Then my wish was actually right.

Richie Obi (10)
Brookfields Primary School, Hockley

My Holiday Journey

We get to the airport quickly and early
And wheel the suitcases firmly

Get to check-in nice and early, first in the queue
The line behind us is long, I just know.

After check-in comes security
And again, the line is long and tumbly.

But I don't mind because soon I will be on the plane
Flying to Spain.

An hour later, we are up in the sky
Up high.

Later, we are on the ground and we rush to get off
To the cabs.

Now we are tired and want our rest
I go to sleep with a smile on my face, thinking, *here is the best.*

Ameelah Plummer
Brookfields Primary School, Hockley

The Flying Dragons

In my dreams every night,
I could see different animals that had the same style as dragons,
They flew through the sky in fire caves,
As if breathed its eyes sparkled
And it glanced at me and looked happy.
One dragon then another passed by me,
In the adventure, the dragons went somewhere.
I found them and sneakily sneaked up on them,
I saw a cave, I was scared but I still went in.
I saw a baby dragon,
I grabbed it and played with it.
I kept it at home as my own pet.
I made a lot of dragon friends
And then I went to my family to tell them what happened.

Robina Katawazai (8)
Brookfields Primary School, Hockley

Dream Of A Fairy

I am a fairy with colourful clothes,
I find myself where the green grass grows,
And where a fine stream flows.

Purple lips like the evening sun,
My words move fast like a Gatling gun,
Eyes twinkle like the morning dew,
No one in the world as beautiful as Muh.

I sit under a swallow's tree,
Watching the leaves of all,
Feeling so calm and free,
Waiting for the night to call.

I start to sing deep,
Everything is as perfect as it seems,
I awake as the morning sun rises,
So this is the fairy - the fairy of my dream.

Hafsa Rahat (9)
Brookfields Primary School, Hockley

What's The Dream Today?

Today, my dream is everything in my head,
Being a famous ballerina, a builder, a monster explorer or an astronaut.
Everything in my head is like little people's big dreams.
This is a real dream with everyone in this world,
Marie Curie, Michelle Obama, Malala Yousafzai, Zaha Hadid, Pelé, Bruce Lee, Frida Kahlo, Elvis Presley and many more people in everyone's dreams.
Forever and ever,
My dreams are never-ending,
My dreams are everything in this world.

Iasmin Ricci (9)
Brookfields Primary School, Hockley

Flowers

F abulous flowers flooded the grass field.
L ooking left to right, all I smell is a fragrant delight.
O ne special flower catches my sight.
W hat will happen if a bee comes out of a bright light?
E verything is bright, unlike the colours of a dark night.
R eaching out for the special flower, I hope the smell doesn't have much power.
S melling the flower with a little bit of fear, and in my bed, I suddenly appear.

Aliya Yusuf (8)
Brookfields Primary School, Hockley

Football

Whenever I play football I feel calm.
My body feels peaceful and happy.
It gives me passion.
Whenever I get out I always want to go to the park
When I score a goal, it gives me that burn that you are a good player.
When you are a keeper and it is a penalty shootout, the team depends on you.
When you save it you celebrate and feel happy.
Football is a game with a lot of this
I would love to play football when I grow up.

David Omosigho (9)
Brookfields Primary School, Hockley

Getting Lost

I am so alone,
I feel so scared,
I am so alone,
I am unprepared.

Getting lost is not a joke,
When you are lost you feel provoked.
Getting lost you are so scared,
When there are other things to bear.

Now I am lost,
I will cry and mope.
In getting lost,
I will have some hope.

Once I was lost,
But now I am found.
But I am not lost again,
I will be around.

Munachi Asidanya (9)
Brookfields Primary School, Hockley

Candy Land

Candy Land, the best in the world
A place no one has ever heard
A place where you and your friends
Can go to take lots of candy home.
Candy, candy everywhere.
Who even knew you were there?
Candy, candy, fill up my tummy
With loads of candy, yum, yum, yummy
Candy, candy over there,
You are the best in the world
Fill up my heart with laughter and joy
See you again next time.

Fatoumatta Ceesay (9)
Brookfields Primary School, Hockley

I Thought About Mother's Day

Our mothers bear our pain
They protect us from the rain
From the day we were small
Till the day we became tall
They gave us wings
And so many rings
One day, she won't be here
So put all those memories in that ear
They are powerful and strong
But sometimes, they make mistakes, and it is okay
I woke up from my dream and thought of how mothers are so wonderful.

Zainab Khizar (10)
Brookfields Primary School, Hockley

The Magical Land

In my dreams every night, trees, grass, flowers
And leaves are all around me.
I am with cute baby rabbits,
Eating grass.
I am in a magical land.
I feel joyful playing with my friends.
I feel shocked because all my magical
Friends are flying.
I am so sad, I really want to fly.
Suddenly I touch myself
And I am flying. I am so happy.

Ahlam Alsasi (9)
Brookfields Primary School, Hockley

Hogwarts' Fantasy

In the midst of the dark, is a cold castle.
Flying high is a broomstick which shines.
In the moonlight are the deadliest monsters,
The Sorting Hat, the most curious wonder.
The train, the fastest car there
The asylum, where you sleep and talk.
Quidditch, a fast little ball.
In the air is a Snitch with a ball.

Omar Osman (9)
Brookfields Primary School, Hockley

A Special Dream!

I can see the most famous footballers in the world.
I'm with Ronaldo and Messi.
We were in a silent, old and empty room.
I was feeling curious, nervous and scared.
When a cheetah was about to jump on us,
My eyes opened and I was in my bed!

Aarush Naresh Kitey (9)
Brookfields Primary School, Hockley

Superheroes

The special abilities superheroes have,
Many can travel at the speed of light,
Also, fly at the speed of light,
Hopefully their favourite is travelling at the speed of light.

Taha Yagoub (9)
Brookfields Primary School, Hockley

Illusion

I've come to the conclusion,
That the world's an illusion
This script is written in our minds,
All the wonders you will find,
Perhaps none of it is real.
The ground, the sky, the entire world,
It all seems like a massive swirl,
The trees the sun, rivers and grass and glimmering stream,
What if it's all just a dream?
Even birds that pass,
The people bustling around the streets,
Only your dreams you truly meet,
It does seem odd to think like this,
I wonder if our imagination has an end,
In front of our eyes is a landscape,
Which only our eyes can shape,
The mind is strange,
The world is just a figment of our imagination,
Simply a neurological creation,
But nothing will ever change,
An illusion the world may be,
But that does not mean you have to stop the discovery!

Lola Wilson (10)
Godmanchester Community Academy, Godmanchester

Fake Reality

Dreaming is cool, sometimes I'm tall,
Sometimes, I'm small,
Sometimes, it's scary,
Sometimes, it's fun,
I can't escape dreams because I'm dumb,
But when I wake up, I'm like, oh, it's just a dream,
And then I want to go right back to sleep.

Theo Oxenbould (10)
Godmanchester Community Academy, Godmanchester

I Am A Dragon

I am a dragon,
I breathe fire as hot as the sun.
My talons destroy all ancient wagons.
You should watch me fight,
It is such a sight.
I give people an amazing fright.
Imagine dragons soaring over us elegantly in the moonlit sky.
What a sight!

Arthur Jupe (10)
Godmanchester Community Academy, Godmanchester

Me And My Pet Monster

M y pet monster lives with me
E erie eyes glow in the dark

A scary growl is beneath my bed
N othing can prepare me for this moment
D awn is nearby, it haunts my pet monster every single night

M y monster hugs me, terrified
Y ummy cupcakes calm my monster

P etrified, my monster hides under the covers because dawn is nearby
E very time my monster's scared, I'm scared with him
T ime is running by

M e and my monster are scared, ten minutes till dawn
O nions are my monster's favourite treat
N ow
S econds go by, my monster is getting scarier and scarier
T errifyingly, he hugs me
E very second, I hear a creak
R ight now, my monster hugs me till it's night again.

Ellie Peone (7)
Goffs Oak Primary School, Goffs Oak

Narrow Escape

In the depths of the forest a boy called Casper did roam,
Curiosity leading him far away from home.
He stumbled upon a peculiar sight;
A delicious-looking fruit in the sunlight.
Casper could not resist and took a big bite,
Gasping loudly with full delight.
But what was happening? Casper was shrinking.
Oh no, a magical berry! he started thinking.
In seconds Casper became only an inch tall.
He was now miniscule compared to them all.
Suddenly, a ginormous ant came into view.
Casper shrieked, "I don't know what to do!"
He started running with all his might,
His freedom worth the risky flight.
With every step, Casper's hope grew dim,
As the ant's shadow loomed over him.
Suddenly, a dragonfly came swooping from the air,
Grabbing Casper by his golden locks of hair.
They flew out of the forest, fast and free;
The boy looked down, amazed by what he could see.
Exhausted, Casper felt sleepy and closed his eyes,
As the dragonfly flew towards the skies.

But he kept on hearing a familiar sizzling sound
Of frying eggs and bacon in the background.
Then his nostrils filled with a smell of coffee with cream.
He opened his eyes... And realised it was just a strange dream.

Casper White (8)
Goffs Oak Primary School, Goffs Oak

Getting Lost

One morning, I woke up and I,
Went to look at the bright morning sky.
Instead of seeing rainbows, the birds or the sun,
I banged my head and dreamt of some fun,
I found myself in a magical place,
I was worried and scared, looking through my hands on my face.
Flying unicorns, a treasure box with wings,
Filled with jewellery and gold and wonderful things.
Tiny little fairies, each with a tiny little light,
We soon became friends and danced through the night.
We danced and in this faraway land,
Then the cutest of the fairies grabbed me by the hand.
She looked into my eyes, to say goodbye,
I didn't know the way home but I knew I had to try.
In the distance by a colourful, magical tree
I saw a unicorn and I knew it was for me.
We flew up high and I started to believe
Anything is possible that you want to achieve.
As the unicorn lowered me into my bed
I felt Mummy kiss me on my head.

"I love you Alessia," and she cuddled me tight.
"God bless you darling, sweet dreams and goodnight."

Alessia McDonald (7)
Goffs Oak Primary School, Goffs Oak

My Dream Zoo

The roar of the lion slowly awakens my senses,
As I drift off to sleep at night,
The chatter of monkeys enhances my smile,
As I wake in my home for the night.

The sound of a slithering snake,
The chuffing of a lone tiger,
The squawk of a colourful parrot,
These sounds bring my new world alive.

The sight of a monochrome zebra,
The view of the penguins playing,
The glimpse of the shy binturong,
Seeing these beautiful animals makes me happy.

The feel of the scales on a lizard,
The touch of the porcupine's quills,
The nudge of the elephant's trunk,
These feelings I long to know.

In my dream, I am roaming a zoo after hours,
When the animals have calmness and quiet.
I can observe their natural behaviours,
Until the sun rises and awakens me from sleep.

Sophie Georgou (8)
Goffs Oak Primary School, Goffs Oak

Fairy

One day I found some fairy dust.
I picked it up, I must!
It turned me into a fairy,
I must say, it was a little bit scary.
I saw my reflection in the mirror,
Pointy ears, sparkly wings, and I used to be bigger.
My dog saw me and started to chase,
And I ran into my pencil case.
I waited till he was fast asleep,
I climbed out of the window into the night sky.
Oh my goodness, I could fly!
I saw my friends, they were just like me.
All flying around like little bumblebees.
Getting tired, I found somewhere to rest my head.
Then I woke up cosy in my bed.
Looking down I realise I am me,
Guess what? It was just a dream.

Evangeline Christofi (8)
Goffs Oak Primary School, Goffs Oak

Transforming Northern Lights

In my dream tonight
I see the Northern Lights
In the sky, at such great height
So colourful and bright

Suddenly they turn blue
And I see London Zoo
It pulls me up into the sky
Then along the Northern Lights I fly

Then I slowly drift down
And see a lion with a crown
In the trees a monkey swings
While flamingos flap and preen their wings

I see the Northern Lights again
And slowly fly up like a plane
I end up in a magic wood
I feel confused but also good.

Where I land I see a fairy
It turns to say follow me.
The Northern Lights start to twist,
Into a sky of bright green mist.

Next I float up to the moon,
Then go down to my bedroom.
The Northern Lights are my view
Surely this could not be true?

Jessica Gray (8)
Goffs Oak Primary School, Goffs Oak

The Dragon And The Sun

In the magic forest
Far, far, away
Dragons were sleeping
Until the sunny May
Unicorns guarded them
From the magic spiders
They were desperately trying
To steal their superpowers
When the time comes
Fairies will appear
Bring the happiness again
And send away the fear
The leader dragon woke up
And immediately started to fly
To see in the ground what was going on
Flying up in the sky
And then he saw the unicorns
Playing and laughing
Teaching the spiders
With fairies how to dance
Then he started to laugh so loud
Making funny noises.
And all the creatures looked straight up

Leaving their toys
It was only a bad dream
Dragon realised
And he was happy that the sun finally arrived.

Despina Chanoglou (8)
Goffs Oak Primary School, Goffs Oak

Football Is Like Working With Your Team

Black and white, you look about,
Football is my fate for life.
Humongous green pitches, you fly around,
This gives you joy when the bright sun is out.
Football is a lot of fun, only if you know how to run, shoot and score a hat-trick, so everyone can see you fly high.

Kick off the game with heads or tails,
Wait and see who's winning the game.
Football is a lot of fun,
So please everyone, enjoy and have fun.

Striker and goalkeeper, defence and midfield, I love them all, so I just can't choose,
Mindblowing goals make the whole crowd go wild,
Saves that wanna make you shout, "Save!"

Mehmet A (8)
Goffs Oak Primary School, Goffs Oak

Once Upon A Dream...

Once upon a dream I see
A football net and a gold trophy
Cheering and chanting, calling my name
Winning goal scored by me, hooray.

Once upon a dream I am
The greatest footballer in all the land
Signing my signature, fans wanting more
Holding the amazing Ballon d'Or.

Once upon a dream I play
Fortnite Battle Royale for days
Fighting and sniping, looting and shooting
"Victory Royale!" I hear you whooping.

Once upon a time I dare
To tumble and turn and flip in the air
Like a peregrine falcon I zoom with speed
I'm the fastest creature in dreams guaranteed.

Stefan Vourloumic (8)
Goffs Oak Primary School, Goffs Oak

Orangutans

O range orangutans swing from luscious trees
R aging, screaming, hunting for their delicious, tasty tea
A mazing orangutans quietly whisper to me
N ow come with me and you'll be in a world of imagination for eternity
G igantic talking rhinos wearing fantastic football kits
U sher us to play their game of soccer where the tall trees sit
T ime is nearly up before I have to say goodbye
A nother adventure into this spectacular, magnificent jungle filled with magic
N ext time I see you will be in a year. Isn't that tragic?
S ee you then my special friend.

Bentley Barclay (8)
Goffs Oak Primary School, Goffs Oak

Sweet Dreams

S tanding in front of me is a mysterious creature
W ith kind eyes and a soft smile, what could it be?
E legant it is, on land or in the sea
E nchanting and magical, what are you?
T errified when I first saw you, but now I'm not scared anymore

D reams are happy with you in them
R ambunctious and playful, you are perfect to me
E verything I've ever wished for in a dream
A nything I do, you do it too, like best friends do!
M y love for you is as strong as the light from the sun
S ea lion, you are so special, I will never forget you.

Sienna Demetriou (8)
Goffs Oak Primary School, Goffs Oak

Dark Dream

D ark, musty, brown-grey walls surround you.
A s you look to the side of the wall you see skulls and abandoned toys,
R usty corners and cracks, spiders coming out of the darkness,
K notty and gnarled wood on the walls,

D reamy, pink sparkles flutter out from a corner, you notice a pixie,
R ainbow colours dance around, the pixie did a spin,
E legantly she danced, but accidentally made a hole in the wall,
A ncient spiders climbed out,
M yself and the pixie jumped on them as they emerged from the cracks, we had escaped!

Sylvie Brandy (8)
Goffs Oak Primary School, Goffs Oak

The Mermaid Mystery

I closed my eyes and fell asleep,
And drifted off to sea,
My tail flicking in the waves,
With my merman cousin Charlie.

We swam around, having fun,
We were not scared or afraid,
Our home was cosy under the sea,
For our family of mermaids.

Suddenly, out of nowhere,
Our faces turned white and pale,
Coming towards us, through the crowds,
Was an angry-looking snail.

He told us, "Go to the real world!
Find snails just like me,
Become a human for evermore,
Make new memories and set your dream free."

Chloe C (8)
Goffs Oak Primary School, Goffs Oak

Dinosaur

D inosaurs are real, they are everywhere I look,
I can see them in the distance, in the jungle and on the beach,
N ow I must move closer to see if you are friendly,
O ff I go on an adventure I have not done before,
S cared and alone, I see a raptor staring at me,
A hand goes out with food and hope,
U nable to move, they slowly approach, taking the food from my hand,
R iding on my new friend's back, my fear of dinos that were never here.

Grace Steel (8)
Goffs Oak Primary School, Goffs Oak

My Dream

Curled up in my hay,
I snooze the day away.
Green grass all around,
I scuttle free across the ground.
The rustling of the trees
And buzzing of the bees.
Life is happening all around me.
I hitch a ride on a magical butterfly over the rainbow
And through the clouds.
I feel so happy, I squeak so loud,
Squeeeeak!
Suddenly, there's darkness,
I am freed from a hand,
Back to the real world,
From a magical land!

Lara Djelil (8)
Goffs Oak Primary School, Goffs Oak

The Magical Forest

Let's go deep down into the forest.
I heard that there are magical things.
I can ride a unicorn.
I can do what I want,
Because this is a dream.
Now, here is the made-up moonshine flower,
It glows with purple light.
Now, let's go,
What other things will we find?
Like the white rocks that smell like chocolate.
Now there's something I'm missing,
My eyes need to say goodbye,
There will be another time to dream.

Alessia Antoniou (8)
Goffs Oak Primary School, Goffs Oak

My Dolphin Holiday

I can't believe this isn't real,
I can believe how happy I feel!
I am on a Center Parcs holiday,
And there are twenty dolphins wanting to play!

Waves crash,
Dolphins splash,
We play and swim all day!

We swim the lazy river for miles,
I see lots of dolphin smiles!
It feels so warm and very sunny,
Dolphins are playful and so funny.

Waves crash,
Dolphins splash,
My amazing dolphin dream!

Ryan Henry-Macklin (8)
Goffs Oak Primary School, Goffs Oak

The Dream Team

I like scoring with a ball into the back of the net.
I'm cheering with my friends and family.
I'm happy because we won the trophy and the medal.
Then I go through to the next stage.
I am excited to play again,
And win again and also win again.
Argh! I feel shocked because I've never done it before.
Grass is soft and I feel like I've won it all.
I want to be a famous winner at football.

Emre Kargi (8)
Goffs Oak Primary School, Goffs Oak

Witches And Wizards

W itches and wizards flying around,
I can't get out!
T he potions and tricks are colourful and magical.
C olours of potions and tricks are everywhere.
H ear the sound of zaps one by one!
E erie noises come out at night.
S uddenly, I'm being chased by snakes, but luckily, I'm in a dream!

Sienna Tse (8)
Goffs Oak Primary School, Goffs Oak

Fairies

F loating in my deepest dream
A iry and light, I feel free
I have wings that sparkle bright
R emembering that I don't have height
I wonder where this will take me
E very dream has a great journey
S ee you soon, my fairy friends, we will meet tomorrow again.

Maria Georgiades (8)
Goffs Oak Primary School, Goffs Oak

Dream Big

I dream big every night
The Rugby World Cup in my sight
My name in lights
Shining big and bright
Crowds cheering my name
I'm sure my life will never be the same
I don't ever want this feeling to end
But sadly it's time to wake up now my friend.

Roman Winter (8)
Goffs Oak Primary School, Goffs Oak

Aliens

A liens hiding under my bed
L iving in fear in my head
I n my dreams, you feel real
E ven when I know I should just chill
N ever again do I want to see you
S cary monsters in my dreams.

Sophia Georgiades (8)
Goffs Oak Primary School, Goffs Oak

Then It Went Dark

One night, in my bed,
Something unusual came into my head.
In a world of clouds, I did meet,
Dancing candyfloss and other sweets.
Then it went dark...
Suddenly, I saw something I'll never fail to remember,
Saying something stupid in front of the teacher!
Everyone laughed apart from me,
Suddenly I felt as small as a pea.
Then it went dark...
I woke up in Hastings 1066,
And a great battle was taking place,
In fighting, I'm not ace,
For it is my greatest fear,
Dying in battle is not fun, I swear!
While fighting in battle I was feeling blue,
I had now died, but was it true?
No, I am snug in my room!
I check my watch, it says 8:33,
Oh no! My second greatest fear is approaching...
I'll be late for school!

Qasim Ali (8)
Hampton Hill Junior School, Hampton Hill

The Midnight Walk

Once you have your torch you think,
I won't be scared or terrified
By what lurks behind that tree.

But you will, I tell you now,
Because there is no going back.
Gather now my friends because the forest is thick,
You start to stumble with your pair and start to think,

"Oh no, oh no, this is a shrine!"
With nothing but you, you start to shake,
You see a demon, white in the face,
Then shout, "Oh light of day, this is my death!"

You try to find your class but it has gone,
Because it has found its way around
To the place where you should have met,
You can't find that place,
So you are lost for evermore.

Your teammate says, "Look at those signs!"
So you follow them and find
That every creak, you think you're going to die,
Then you say, "This is the way!"

You find your class and go back home,
Knowing that you will never be alone.

Federico Orlando (10)
Hampton Hill Junior School, Hampton Hill

It All Starts With A Dream

After a long day, full of work and play,
It's time to lie down and let your worries go away,
Do your last things, it's time to rest and sleep,
Time to lie down, don't stir or peep.

Some dreams are good, like counting sheep,
Or being a whale living in the deep,
Some are about pirates sailing the seas,
And some are about unicorns being free.

Some dreams are bad, about witches and hags,
Some are about embarrassing moments when you get nagged,
Some are about monsters under the bed,
Some are about the ghosts of the long dead.

Luckily, you'll have good ones,
But you'll also have bad ones,
Some of them you don't know you've had,
So count one, two, three and then once upon a dream.

Ammar Ali (10)
Hampton Hill Junior School, Hampton Hill

One Mysterious Onyx Night

One night it was a dark night. A kid was walking home. Suddenly, there was a thunderstorm. Creatures flew out of the storm. This all started in the forest. He was terrified to the next level. Now all he could see were monsters. His pet dragon flew out of the sky, swooping him up. Then they got shot out of the sky. Mysteriously, he found a few spirit pots and sucked them into the pots. The monsters used mind control to turn his pet against him. Then, magically, a wizard turned it to day and all the creatures vapourised in the sunlight. All he had left of his dragon was its ashes that he buried in a pot that said 'Once lived'. He hoped that would happen again at Easter with sweets, chocolate and Easter cakes bright and early.

Jesse Turner (9)
Hampton Hill Junior School, Hampton Hill

The Dream Catcher

Every night as I lie in bed a magic world appears in my head,
I wander down the Hall of Dreams and see what awaits me.
I go to the dream room,
Which is filled with happiness, not one bit of gloom,
I make the dreams with just the right amount of dream fire.
I mix them up and send them through the dream tubes
And off to different bedrooms.
I have a dream library where I can make my dreams into books and a dream den where I can float on clouds of happiness and into the sky.
I fly and swing around magical worlds of dreams that gleam.
I go to my bedroom in this magic world
And I fall asleep once more,
I wake up this morning right back at home
And go downstairs for breakfast.

Jacob Hollis (10)
Hampton Hill Junior School, Hampton Hill

Dreamy Sleep

As I lie down in my bed
Magical thoughts start to fill my head
And as I drift off to dreamy sleep
These enchanted moments are mine to keep

A beautiful woodland catches my eye
So I creep a little closer to have a spy
And there before me are glowing flowers
So magical that they give me powers

Suddenly, I'm engulfed in this magical whirl
Whilst dancing fairies twirl and swirl
The sound of wizards laughing and having fun
Makes me wonder how this all began

This really is the happiest place
Every fairy has a smile on their face
Where flowers glow and stars shine bright
I wish I could be here every night.

Isabella Richardson (8)
Hampton Hill Junior School, Hampton Hill

Creepy Pirates

C reeping cautiously out of bed
R ealising I'm on a boat instead
E xtra careful. Wait, who's that man with an
E yepatch? And there's a sailor with a
P eg leg!
Y ikes! Look, there's another with a

P arrot! They're battered, fearsome pirates
I feel seasick in the tummy
R um bottles in their hands as one bellows
"A rrh me matey! Walk the plank!"
T rembling with fear I walk down the
E ndless plank! I reach the end and topple off. "Arghh!"
S uddenly, I am back in my cosy bed.

Meg Porteous (9)
Hampton Hill Junior School, Hampton Hill

Roller Coaster Rush

"Come on Meg, on we get,
This one will be the best one yet!"
Climbing, creeping, up the track,
Up we go, no turning back!

Holding tight, sweaty hands,
Sizzling hot like frying pans,
Smiling faces all around,
But I want my feet back on the ground.
Plunging down the vertical drop,
Wait! Wait! Make it stop!
The track ahead is running out,
"Let me go! Let me go!" I shout!
Here we go, we are going to crash!
Back in bed as quick as a flash!
"How did that happen?" I said.

Eleanor Porteous (9)
Hampton Hill Junior School, Hampton Hill

The Leaves Are An Inferno!

The leaves are an inferno
Roaring red leaves
Swaying on the branch
With many leaves next to it
And the trees breaking

The leaves are an inferno
Dropping leaves are tumbling
Like birds flying out of their nest
Leaves are elegantly dancing
Gracefully like a ballet dancer

The leaves are an inferno
Fiery, red leaves are sunbathing
Like a pan of bacon
The carpet of orange leaves is a crackling carpet
On the ground

The yellow, crisp, crackling leaves are going to sleep.

Ahmed Abani (9)
Hampton Hill Junior School, Hampton Hill

Dreams, Dreams, What Can You Be?

In my dreams every night,
Dreams whizz upon my head.
I can see fairies dancing across the moonlit sky,
Famous dancers flying across the floor,
Dragons having superpowers throughout the day,
Wizards getting lost between the moon and sun,
Famous footballers being royalty forever and ever,
Astronauts finding the Eco Nebula,
Teachers learning lots of interesting things,
I hope I get more dreams.

Dia Tandon (8)
Hampton Hill Junior School, Hampton Hill

A Dream That Will Not Be Forgotten In Years

Dreams, they're all around us
Sleeping, imagining, thinking on the bus
Maybe on an elephant's tusk!
But what I know now and what you may know
Our heads always and always know dreams are something.
That make happiness come...
Have you heard my dreams?
Here's one...
My dad loved fishing
But I loved dippin' my chicken nuggets
My mum loved shoes
Don't know why
But my brother wants to move
I hope we won't
But the very next day
They say we will not stay
And we go
I wish I could say no
When we got to our new house

Our cat made friends
With a rat and mouse!
But then I realised
It is a dream...
There you go
A poem, a dream
And maybe a scheme
But that's a story
That's ridiculous
But here's a real poem!
Flying cows,
Adorable meows,
And even a quiet town
But the sun has a burner
With no burns,
The moon is very soon
Getting his wish come true
But the clouds are playing right now
So don't worry about rain
There's none of it
We've saved the Earth
Just chilling
The birds are nippin'
On the worm
Who used to live in a stern

So now you know why
Poems are incredible.

Henry Hall (9)
Kennall Vale School, Truro

You Will Find Out

Once, I found myself waking up in a school. When I stood up, I saw someone in front of me. I was trying to get past. When I was walking, I turned around to see the person but she wasn't there, so I looked forward but there the person was, right in front of me! They were smiling at me, and not in a nice way, but in a creepy way.

I saw that the person was drooling and I knew that she was going to eat me. I ran towards the wall because there was a portal. When I came out I saw multiple people surrounding me. So, I looked in my pocket to see if there was anything useful, but all I found was a mini CD player, so I played it.

All of the people surrounding me had gone to the first one. So, I kept looking around the school and I found a closet, so I opened it and found a human called Lottie and she asked me what my name was. I told her it was Lilly. Before I could escape we had to get weapons to defeat the drooling monsters.

We found some monsters were not moving so Lottie and I got really suspicious. We stared at them for quite a while. When we blinked the monsters were in a frog pose and killed Lottie!

Freya TS (9)
Kennall Vale School, Truro

Elements

Fire
Flickering, flaming, sending cinders through the air.
Fire is power, I can assure you, it's only fair.
When it's lit, there is smoke in the breeze,
And everybody is at ease when fire is at peace.

I know the spirits of fire are watching over us.
For we believe in fire.
And there is some kind of fire that lives inside us.
For fire, is passion, bravery and mind.

Water
We splish, we splash, we could play all day.
We splosh, we splish, we run away.
Attacking, retreating, the tide is coming in.
Some stuff in the water should go in the bin!

Earth
You can thank the ground for what you have.
Crystal, iron and vegetation, we're not that bad.
Uranium, titanium and tungsten, we've got it all.
And we haven't told you everything you need to know.
We are tough and some of us glow.

Air
The wind helps the bees, birds and bugs.
And sometimes we can give you a tug.
My friends and I will fly all day,
Playing and dazing in the clouds
Rising, rising, ever so high,
Rising, rising, time to say bye.

Edan Fyffe (9)
Kennall Vale School, Truro

My Dreamland

Whoosh! Bang! Crash!
I fell down, I thought it was the end,
And then I felt something break my fall...

For a few moments, I was absorbed in a soft monster eating me,
It started to feel like time itself stopped.

But then everything started racing and became blurry.

The ground was shaking, terror was rising.

I shut my eyes...

My Dreamland stole me,
Took me to Dreamland,
It's free,
It is special,
The place where you can unleash your powers,
Have fun for hours.

Be yourself in Dreamland.
I saw magical creatures,
Should I be scared?;
I said hi,
And they understood me.

Wow.
Time to go. No, I will stay for a bit longer.
Wow! I know you, I've seen you on TV.
Please can I have your autograph? Yes. Yes!
I love Dreamland. Leaving now, time to wake up...
Beep. Beep. Beep. Beep
Morning now. Goodbye Dreamland, see you soon.

Ayla P (9)
Kennall Vale School, Truro

Floating Through The Air

Floating through the air, birds fly upon me. I fly happily across the clouds and I stop sometimes to collect some candyfloss. I trudge along the clouds with my fabulous family.

Then I fly with my family, passing by different lands taking in the beautifulness. But wait, I have found a sweet and chocolate land. Oh my gosh, I go flying around the place with my dog, collecting it all. It is like nothing I have ever done before. The sweets glisten and the chocolate shines and it is as brown as dirt. The birds tweet like Ed Sheeran. We keep on flying, shooting past our buddies and playing games. As we fly, birds' feathers brush across the tips of my hair.

As we go back home we eat all the sweets and play all the video games, winning them all. Then we all settle down on the fresh, pitch-white cloud sofa, eating every last crumble of the chocolate and the sweets.

Jude (9)
Kennall Vale School, Truro

My Dream Cornwall

Seagulls, seagulls flying everywhere.
Seagulls pooping in your hair.
They steal your food, they are very rude
And we wish they were subdued.

Pasties are our favourite thing to eat.
They are very delicious with the meat.
Hot or cold, they are a tasty treat
That we don't want to drop on our feet.

Clotted cream is all the craze.
You can eat it in many ways.
Ice cream, coffee or afternoon tea
But please don't drop it in the sea.

The weatherman says it's going to be sunny.
Oh, it's raining and it's not funny.
The holidaymakers are all wet
Including their wet, soggy pets.

But the sun will be out tomorrow
So dry those tears and no more sorrow.
Cornwall is a happy place
And you can see it on everyone's face.

Beau Main (9)
Kennall Vale School, Truro

Dinosaur Island

I was in a forest with trees,
The bark was brown, dark brown,
And I saw a dinosaur with blood
Dripping from its razor-sharp teeth
Which could cut straight through bone!
The mud sloshed underneath my feet,
The mud looked like a muddy puddle,
But more sticky.

All of a sudden, a stegosaurus
Poked out of a tree,
Giving me a heart attack.
When I woke up,
I had slobber falling on my face
From the stegosaurus.

On this island there were poisonous berries,
If you ate one, you would survive,
But you would be sick for a year.

Some of the dinosaurs had sharp claws,
That would rip your flesh out,
And you won't live to see
Another day.

Brachiosaurus is the tallest dinosaur,
It will flatten you like a pancake. *Splat!*

Aubrey French (9)
Kennall Vale School, Truro

The School For Monsters And Villains

Once upon a time, there was a girl called Alice (me) and my friends, called Chloe and Cleo. We were walking to our new secondary school. We were so confused because the school was black and grey. It was so dull that it frightened us to death.
So we opened the door and looked inside. It was a school full of hideous creatures. We were so scared. So we turned around and pondered how we could turn into ugly monsters to be at this school.
Two minutes later we came up with a beautiful plan. It was to do make-up, nails and costumes. Mine was a wolf, but purple, and Choe and Cleo's was a butterfly and a pink witch.
When we walked to classes we noticed we had lockers and the lockers were green for the boys and purple for the girls. They were plain so, well, guess what we did? We... decorated them!

Ayla R (10)
Kennall Vale School, Truro

A Mystery

I woke up inside a dark room, my eyes stung from the night before. As I sat up, I realised I was sitting on a pale white bed. It was like sitting on a bed of rocks. Next door, I smelt the stench of rotten apples. "Ew, what's that smell? Where am I?" As I looked up at the walls and ceiling I could see a sort of mossy tinge to both of them. All of the little creases were completely black just like the colour of midnight.

I thought of my parents, *where are they? I don't know, are they worried?* I started walking around the room. Oh no! I was locked in! What was I going to do now? It was almost dawn. I paced on down, my heart beating fast. The smell was getting worse now. It was so bad I could hardly breathe. "Hello, anyone?" Oh phew! It was just a dream.

Ailla Mulhern (9)
Kennall Vale School, Truro

The Sunflower Field

Dream, dream, dream...
Run away far, far away,
Through sunflower fields and rushing aqua rivers.
I am lying in the lush emerald grass,
Running in the trees,
And feeling the cold breeze,
In my face.
I go swimming in the untamed rivers,
And I let my spirit protect me at my own risk.

I am not letting my imagination get the better of me,
This is my world.
This is like my dream come to life,
The animals in this fantasy are from beautiful red forests,
To sapphire-blue butterflies.
When I am running, I feel free,
Each stroke of light on the sunflower leaves,
Fills me with love.

I will stay here through spring,
Summer,
Autumn,
And winter...
This is my dream,
In the sunflower field.

Lottie W (9)
Kennall Vale School, Truro

Candy World

There's a wolf made out of candy,
It's running around like a cheetah,
Hang on, did you just eat the candy wolf?
Anyway, I went into the candy house,
There were biscuits and lollipops,
I took a bite out of it,
There was a biscuit wall,
It was very yummy.
I finally got out of the candy house,
And then I took a bite out of that.
It tasted nice, so I took another.
I couldn't stop so I ate a hole in the candy tree,
It was so yummy.
I explored Candy World,
I tried the candy grass and a candy leaf,
Until I hit a candy boat,
So I went into the candy boat,
I explored Candy World
On the candy sea
And then I hit a candy village
There were candy houses in it.

Elliot S (8)
Kennall Vale School, Truro

Do Rivers Have Secrets?

Last night, I dreamt of a river,
Her name was The River Of Life,
She flows through me,
She dances through you,
As she sings to the sky above.

I ran to this sacred place,
Where she listened to my secrets,
She set me free to the world,
She kept my spirit and soul safe,
As I listened to her welcoming voice.

And then one night, I was lost and scared,
But she danced and darted through the trees,
Until darkness fell, black as coal,
But not for the mother moon,
Shining down on her glistening daughter.

The River of Life has so many secrets,
Flowing through her veins,
As her sapphire hair beams off the sun so bright,
I wake up hoping to see her again.

Oriole L (10)
Kennall Vale School, Truro

The Koala

One day, there was a koala. He lived in Australia in a house full of candy. The door was covered in chocolate. He had a tree in his garden and he was ominously sitting in it. He glistened his sky-blue eyes and could scream as loud as a drum. His friends came and said, "Do you want to play with us?"
"No," he screamed as loud as a drum.
The candy burped. The friends said, "Pardon you."
He tried to see if he could get down. He was astonished that he could climb down. He said to his friends, "Wait."
"I thought you did not want to play with us."
"Well, now I do."
"Okay."
He went with his friends.

Hugo Z (9)
Kennall Vale School, Truro

The Tiger Sun

Timing, timing, must hurry
Got to see the sun rising
Got to see the tiger sun
Hurry, hurry! Up the hill, got to see the sun

Instant, instant, must hurry
Got to see the sun rising
Got to see the tiger sun
Hurry, hurry! Up the tower, got to see the sun

Go, go, tiger sun but don't be late for me
I will hang on until you go for tea

Enter, enter with your tiger sun
Come in,
I will give you breakfast with lots of sunshine

Rise, rise, go back to your place in the sky
All the folk miss you
I think they might cry.

Jamie T (9)
Kennall Vale School, Truro

My Dream Land

My dream land is rainbow ponds, flowers,
But mainly cats. I love cats.
The sky is as blue as tropical seas,
Coconuts and mangos falling from trees,
No cars, lots of animals and creatures,
Smiles everywhere you look,
The smiles spread like wildfire,
Sun shining on your face, spreading rays of warmness.

Travel, travel around the land, far and wide,
Kitties bouncing like kangaroos,
Flowers dancing in the light wind,
Trees blossoming, colours blooming all around,
I love it here and so will you!

This is my dream... in Cat Land.

Ella Thompson (9)
Kennall Vale School, Truro

Dream Wood

This is my dream wood
I used to visit it so much, as much as I could
There are bees and flowers
And I can relax for hours

I like to watch light dance through trees
That's the best bit about dreams
There are no rules
You can fly through the sky or swim in a pool

You could ride on a wolf
Or watch owls hoot
You could sleep in a box
Or tickle a fox

Dreams are like flowers
You could have any powers
They could blossom out at any time
That's why I like to sit here among the pines.

Layla Young (10)
Kennall Vale School, Truro

The Mad Inventor

The mad inventor is a biscuit,
A gingerbread body, with crazy hair,
His creation - a lava dog mixed with a wolf!
A pointy-eared (and grey) animal.
The biscuit turned his friend into a dog.
A good friend, friend no longer,
He took him to a castle,
A castle guarded by screaming heads,
Dark and gloomy,
A forgotten fortress of death,
An eerie castle with a clown stuck in a prison,
Cold and dark,
Their cries masked by the thick walls,
Oh to be saved,
His minions were little fluffy one-eyed dolls.

Isolde R (9)
Kennall Vale School, Truro

My Dream

I'm in my bedroom.
I have a rainbow-coloured keyboard, mouse, mouse pad,
40-inch TV and three monitors which are behind me
That leads to a secret room.
The room contains all of my friends.
LEDs light up the room like a glow worm.
My cat, Figi, wanders in and out of the secret room with a treat dispenser
That dispenses treats every hour.
As she leaves,
She climbs on the fabric wall and onto her Total Wipeout course -
With a bowl of wet food waiting for her at the end.

Eli E (10)
Kennall Vale School, Truro

Sea Monkeys

Sea monkeys are common novelty aquarium pets.
Sea monkeys are shy omnivores.
Sea monkeys eat algae and shrimp.
Sea monkeys are known for their unique lifecycle.
Sea monkeys have only one eye when they hatch.
But by the time they're fully grown, they have three eyes.
Sea monkeys grow up to ½ to ¾ inches in length.
Sea monkeys were developed in the USA in 1957.
When sea monkeys are fully grown they are 6-12 years old.
Sea monkeys swim about forever.

Elijah Wickes (9)
Kennall Vale School, Truro

Poems Galore

P oems galore, circle around me,
O n the floor, the police found me,
E very time it hurts my head,
M um, please, can't I come home to bed?
S omeone down there will probably miss their family.

G oing to New York to meet Fred.
A t the city, they will share a kiss,
L aughed my head off,
O ver the bridge was a drop,
R evive me, said the king,
E ver thought of a new city?

Rowan P
Kennall Vale School, Truro

My Dream Pet

Cute, fluffy and clean, it will clean itself in one lick. They are great as pets and they love to play in the sun, on a boring, wet day they don't like to play and they will sleep on your lap all winter. When they wake up from their slumber they will need to eat and drink. They are a lot of responsibility, you know you have to pay attention. One is okay but two is better. They like a lot of company. The pet is a chinchilla!

Lyra C (9)
Kennall Vale School, Truro

The Nightmare

I woke up in a cold sweat. It appeared last night. Its breath was on my neck, sending a chill down my spine, enduring the few seconds between wake and sleep. As I woke, its fingers were touching my neck, allowing air into my lungs again. Finally, my gasp sprang my eyelids open only to be confronted by the inky black stains left on the silky walls. My heart pounded as I woke up, but it was just a nightmare.

Jake M (9)
Kennall Vale School, Truro

Dream...

Dreams are funny things
Sometimes they're there and sometimes
They're gone...

They can be about a bus, train, star,
Game or even a purple swan.

Sometimes they come, night or day
They never stay for long.

They can be bad or good, but
You always should dream on and on and on.

Phoebe Young (10)
Kennall Vale School, Truro

Sea Of Monsters

The waves slapped the shore like a giant hand and boxing glove,
A yacht glided onto the beach with a *crash!*
Someone else got crushed into a pancake.
Splat!
In the yacht, another wave punched the sand,
Suddenly a riptide carried the yacht into the sea.
After an hour I couldn't see land.

Joby S (9)
Kennall Vale School, Truro

The Dorm Of Dreams

In the dorm, you can pick the dream you prefer. There's Adventure, Quests and Survival. Oh, and there's an emergency wake-up room.
Wake up! Let's to go my mystical land. What do you want to do here? Do you want to explore?
Hey, look. It's the Universe Tree. Here your thoughts will become reality.

Travis (9)
Kennall Vale School, Truro

The World Of Capybaras

Everywhere I look, I can see capybaras.
There are even ten capybara statues,
Capybara boots,
Capybara T-shirts,
Capybara shops
And clothes.

The world is filled with capybara planes
And cars covered in bandanas.
Capybara world.
Capybaras rule.
My capybara world.

Hugo Meagor (9)
Kennall Vale School, Truro

Something

S omehow the sky turned red,
O ur eyes bled,
M y face was red,
E very time it hurt my head.
T hings ate my head,
H eads weren't fed,
I n the ground people were dead,
N ight unrolled over a red bed,
G rand people fled.

Arthur R (9)
Kennall Vale School, Truro

Oh No, Monster

M e in my room in my bed asleep, my light turns on and I hear someone leap.
"**O** h no!" keeps going around in my head, oh, I feel like there's something near my bed.
N ot my imagination again, I think. Not even scared, even though I wait to blink.
S uddenly I hear footsteps on the floor, sounding like boulders near my bright red door.
T hen appears near my bed a weird monster, the creature looks like a giant lobster!
E nough, so I run and he chases me, I think the end of my life I can see.
R unning for my life, heart beating so fast, really tired, I hope this does not last.
"Somebody, please help me!" I loudly scream. So glad that it was just a really bad dream.

Yashnoor Nahar (10)
Rokeby Primary School, Rugby

People Now Freed

P eople, what on earth are people?
E nthusiastic to find one,
O nly one person in the world,
P ossibly no, it can never be,
L ocating people... impossible!
E ven when I try and try.

N ow I feel I am getting close,
O nly a little while to go,
W hat... I'm getting even further.

F ind a person - I don't think I can
R eally? Well, I don't think I can.
E very day I keep on trying,
E ven though I am losing hope,
D on't underestimate me, people!

Luna Overton (10)
Rokeby Primary School, Rugby

Untitled

M iles of travelling
A crowded city
G etting past thousands of people
I sn't it confusing?
C an't understand
A ll of this is a mistake
L et me free!

S o much chaos!
U nbelievable!
P owers I can't control!
E legant!
R eally on a mission!
P owers are crazy!
O n my own.
W orking hard!
E nd of me, I'm too exhausted.
R eally getting lost!
S orry, time for me to rest.

Victoria Szymala (8)
Rokeby Primary School, Rugby

Back In Time

We've arrived again, back in time,
Earth had a dream, once it was lime...

Rocks and lava hurl through the air,
The moody caveman's deep... dark... lair...

They're frightening creatures bathing in flint,
Look! A dodo, too bad they're extinct!

But no period will ever compare,
To when dinosaurs were covered in hair!

But now it's time to head back,
With my full history sack!

To protect our world while we can,
It's the big 'Save Our Planet' plan!

Connie Barnes (10)
Rokeby Primary School, Rugby

The Eleven-Plus Exam!

E leven-plus, an educational exam,
L earning persistently every day to prepare,
E very time you have a question, say Mam,
V ery much books to care,
E very day, every hour, every second is precious,
N ice, happy smile and you'll have a good day.

P ractising and getting new homework (always ambitious),
L earning and revising very exhausting subjects at the beginning of May,
U nder all of that, have some joy!
S urely you passed, so enjoy!

Muqeet Shaik (10)
Rokeby Primary School, Rugby

People With Dreams

Flying a rocket to the moon,
Racing sports cars and getting on the news,
Making music and going viral,
Riding motorbikes in a circus, in a spiral!

Playing football and becoming famous,
Doing science and making potions,
Becoming a director and making films,
Creating books and illustrations!

Becoming a teacher and helping kids,
Being a parent and raising people,
Being a postman and delivering gifts,
Becoming a popstar and inspiring lots!

Jackson Jewers (9)
Rokeby Primary School, Rugby

When I'm Older

When I'm older,
I've got a dream,
To play a joyful song,
With a crowd like a river stream.

When I'm older,
I'll be happy,
Playing a song,
That makes fans sappy.

When I'm older,
I'll be on stage,
With a band my age,
Looking at a hater with an angry rage.

When I'm older,
I'll have lots of fame,
While my children are doing the same.

Judaea Clarke (8)
Rokeby Primary School, Rugby

My Dream Mansion

Lollipop Land, the lollipops taste like a dance
My roof is a rainbow
My honey is the sunlight
My orchard shines in the sunlight like glass

Cherry flowers glow in the dark
Mint trees shine to the moon
The lollipop country is a hill of treats

Sometimes, the lightning goes flash!
Dripping with grape icing, it was heaven in my mouth
When I woke up, I was tucked up in bed.

Kushi Sachin (8)
Rokeby Primary School, Rugby

The Scariest Dream Ever

One time I had a dream.
I lay in bed, scared and afraid,
But I ignored my worries and I closed my eyes.

A terrible nightmare filled my head,
A dream so full of dread,
A dream where I ended up dead,
A dream where on the floor I bled.
There I stood in the road when I saw a car and I froze.
Crash! It hit me.
And then I woke up from that horrible nightmare.

James Taylor-Gittins (9)
Rokeby Primary School, Rugby

Forgotten

F ighting creatures left and right.
O val teeth, spikes beneath my feet.
R oaring depths of deepest reach.
G ory oceans, bloody streams.
O ccurring disasters, around my eyes.
T owering boulders, smashing trees.
T otal darkness, flowing creeps.
E ternal dullness, creepy creaks.
N ever to be seen in the darkest dream.

Gerald Kanini (9)
Rokeby Primary School, Rugby

Getting Lost

G oing through the forest
E verything is empty
T he howling of the wolves
T he doors lock
I t's the end for me!
N owhere to hide
G oing as fast as I can

L eaving my friend behind to die!
O pening a door
S lamming the door shut
T ime to die.

Sienna Bilby (8)
Rokeby Primary School, Rugby

Cars

Fast cars, around,
A cricket, at high speed,
Around corners.

Fast hits, at high speed,
Brakes getting hot,
High into corners.

Practice is best,
Different countries everywhere,
Different continents.

Some countries have more tracks,
Street tracks everywhere,
Famous tracks somewhere.

Jacob King (9)
Rokeby Primary School, Rugby

The Beautiful Pink World

In the beautiful pink world,
You see the beautiful soft leaves,
Strong leaves with a beautiful pink sky,
With the tiny pink flowers,
With the beautiful bright pink sun
And the pink forest.
World War III was starting,
The water explosion,
The explosion of the sound,
The house explosion.

Kabinin Ibrahim (10)
Rokeby Primary School, Rugby

Teacher

S houting at the kids
'C ause they can,
A ngry and frustrated.
R eally quite overrated.
Y elling.

T urning,
E arning,
A rching,
C heering.
H elping,
E xciting,
R hyming, timing.

Jordyn Crouch (8)
Rokeby Primary School, Rugby

Untitled

I wake up in a spooky place.
Scared to look around me.
I go and go.
I can see a creepy house.
The house is enormous and dark.
Nobody is in there I think.
I go inside to see what's there.
I see an immense, hairy spider.
Then I fall in a portal.
I wake up back at home.

Zawe Salahadin (8)
Rokeby Primary School, Rugby

Superhero

S uperhero
U nbelievable
P rotect innocent people
E rror, "Oh no"
R eady for action
H elp! Help!
E rror, "Again! Oh No,"
R eally again, Joker: "Hehehe, I'm gonna win"
O h no, uh-oh.

Tyanna Beckford (7)
Rokeby Primary School, Rugby

Dreamland

Finally, the end of school was here,
After dinner, I realised sleep was here.
I asked my mum if I could go to sleep,
"Yes," she said, "go away!"
I went without a peep.
Brushed my teeth and went to bed,
When all of a sudden,
A weird dream filled my head.

Henry Gravell (8)
Rokeby Primary School, Rugby

MrBeast

M aster of everything.
R ich and famous.
B raver than a bear.
E ndless money, more than me.
A mazing and shiny.
S uper strong.
T aking and selling Feastibles for homeless kids.

Marlon Walder (8)
Rokeby Primary School, Rugby

Nightmare

Oh no! I am in a weird house,
There are five locks
I hear glass break
And the door lock and the window lock too
But we have to find the key
I keep hearing doors closing
Nooooo...

Edy Soare (9)
Rokeby Primary School, Rugby

Untitled

F antastic house
A mazing life
M arvellous money
O ut of this world
U nique and fascinating
S ometimes, I need to rethink!

Charlie Platt (7)
Rokeby Primary School, Rugby

Famous

F un and flashing lights!
A wesome!
M um not bothering me!
O ut to parties!
U s going shopping!
S ee the cute flower!

Oliver O'Donnell (8)
Rokeby Primary School, Rugby

The Moon And The Star

The sun went to sleep
The moon was smiling at the stars
The stars said hi back to the moon.

Isabel Stanhope (8)
Rokeby Primary School, Rugby

Dream Big

D are to try, don't be afraid.
R ace to the start.
E njoy the time, make each moment count.
A mazing adventures, push away all the doubt.
M emories are made in lots of new things.

B eautiful beginnings.
I nterests explored and found
G reat times to be had and friendships are bound.

Abigail Maisey (9)
Springbank Academy, Eastwood

Dancing In The Dark

Once upon a time, me and my friend were walking in the park just before dark. Everything was normal until we saw a sudden sparkly light in the distance and thought we should take a look.
As we stepped closer, we saw a book and it was sparkling. We hesitated at first, but opened it and... dance music started playing. Two fairies danced and sang until it stopped. We stared at each other. Then suddenly, the fairies started to talk to each other. Then they started to talk to us.
They said, "We have an offer. Will you compete to be the best dancer and see the dancing world?"
We looked at each other and started screaming, "Yes, yes, yes!"
Suddenly, we were sucked into the book and dressed in beautiful dresses. Then we were told to wait for the dance competition. We weren't sure we'd win, but we believed, tried and trained until we fell asleep.
The next morning, a black jeep arrived. We were confused until the fairies came and said it was there to pick us up for the competition.
We said, "Already?!"
They replied, "Yeah!"

In the blink of an eye, we were at the competition. As soon as we got there, we had to dance and dance. We were winning, but all of a sudden, with a little magic and dancing, we made everyone feel like they were in a trance. We won the dance competition and were happy. We got a trophy for winning.

Jemima Kavhu (10)
St Wilfrid's Catholic Primary School, Angmering

The Magic Dream Diary

M y brain switches off as I fall into a deep sleep
A fun day begins when I find a magic diary
G etting excited, I jot down my dream of flying a magic panda to school
I go outside the front door to catch the bus but a panda is there staring at me
C leverly, the panda pushes me and my friends on his back where a pink, sparkling ribbon is on his neck.

D ancing in the sky, he makes me and my friends laugh
R acing in the sky, dodging the clouds
E verywhere we look is like a dream come true
A rriving at school, it is time to say our goodbyes to our best panda buddy
M eeting a panda that'll never forget

D isappointingly, it is time to go to bed and come to the end of an amazing time
I wake up feeling annoyed it was only a dream
A few hours later, I feel weird, so I go and get a drink of water
R unning to my room to check everything's alright, I look under my pillow and there's a pink, sparkling ribbon
Y ou would think I'd know the difference between a dream and real life, but I am not really sure now.

Was this really a dream?

Caitlan Hayler (10)
St Wilfrid's Catholic Primary School, Angmering

The Dragon

My eyes feel weary as I lie in bed,
The warmth of the pillow beneath my head.
The darkness of the night sky,
And the stars bright way up high.
All I was left with was my mind,
So I thought of this:
Once there was a town,
Under the clouds.
A sudden boom of rage filled the air.
Because deep within the dark abyss,
A storm began to brew,
Those above seemed to miss
The chaos that ensued.
A dragon emerged,
Everyone was filled with fear.
But not me because I saw no harm happening here.
So I hopped on its back,
And flew through the clouds,
But then I came back to the ground.
I am now starting to feel the covers of my bed,
And the warmth of the pillow beneath my head.

Amelia Dudley (9)
St Wilfrid's Catholic Primary School, Angmering

Once Upon My Dream

Once upon my dream,
A little while ago,
I had never dreamt before,
So I thought I should have a go.
It was wonderful, really,
Nothing super creepy,
You know,
It was all quite a show.
After I closed my eyes,
I suddenly just rised.
I saw specks of dust,
They kind of looked like rust.
Then I heard a ding,
It went *ring, ring, RING!*
It was just then I realised what was happening,
They were fairies, they were fairies and they all started to sing.
I followed them all the way to a star,
I saw my house from afar.
Just then I suddenly fell!
Into my bed.
Once upon my dream.

Florrie Bloomer (9)
St Wilfrid's Catholic Primary School, Angmering

The Dream To Be

Once upon a time, there was a young boy.
He was eight years old and full of joy.
Footballer was his dream to be,
On the pitch for all to see.
The dream is real,
It makes me feel happy and excited
To be a star in the making,
The crowds are roaring.
I'm really here! I can't believe it
I'm playing a football match,
My dream has come true.
This is where I'm supposed to be happy and free.
I scored a goal, the best one everyone has seen.
Everyone can see that I'm so happy and keen.
After getting Man of the Match
A trophy with gleaming stars,
It's mine to keep for many years.
I don't want the feeling to pass
One day I hope my dream comes true
To be the footballer I wish to be
To feel the happiness I hold,
To feel my heart so full

I'm breathing fast
Will this dream really last?

Kyan Enver (8)
The Discovery School, West Malling

Disneyland

D ancing through the incredible gates of Disneyland
I saw beaming lights in the dark, moonlit sky
S parkling rides with all different colours, twinkling around
N ear the Ferris wheel, I saw a pink, fluffy candyfloss laughing
E ntering the shop, I saw loads of Minnie Mouse headbands as red as rubies
Y elling children on the roller coasters and they shout even louder when they go upside down
L anding at the bottom of the slide I bumped into the most beautiful princess I had ever seen
A fter I opened the huge gates to enter the castle, I covered my mouth at the sight that I saw
N ever did I think I would see a shower of marshmallows *pitter-pattering* onto the ground
D isneyland is the best place ever!

Olivia Read (8)
The Discovery School, West Malling

One Magical Wish

One stressful morning, lived a house, not any house, a dull, dark place. During the nights in my dreams, I wished for lots of powers like flying mysteriously. When I woke up everything was the same, I tried harder during the day. Everything was lovely but not good. One night, my wish was colourful finally.

Happily the next day my whole family got powers. Hopefully next year we will get more powers like invisibility.

The next day was miserable. My family and I lost our powers. We went back to normal. It was plain and boring.

Two days later our powers came back and the friendly unicorn in the sky with flowers in her hair came and visited me. Maybe next year we will get more powers.

Ella Wigg (8)
The Discovery School, West Malling

My Dreamy Future

M y future, I can see it!
Y es, I can see it!

D aydreaming, writing,
R eading, drawing,
E ating fresh, yummy fruit,
A pples, grapes,
M angoes, peaches,
Y es, I see it!

F uture, I love that word.
U nicorns, dragons, fruit aliens, I will write about them all.
T ess Oakley, best-selling children's author and illustrator, oh I can see it.
U nilions, aligons, crococats, I write about them all.
R ead, write, draw, imagine and munch fruit.
E very day.

Tess Oakley (8)
The Discovery School, West Malling

Ponies

P onies flying through the air, giving wishes and hope to everyone.
O n the cloud, we lie down in the cosy softness and look up into space.
N ow the ponies are back on Earth, munching some golden, tasty hay.
I n the countryside, they gallop through the emerald-green fields.
E very night after granting a few wishes, they dream in their paddocks of where their next trip is.
S ome wish for hot countries, some wish for cold, but most wish to relax and find a best friend and belong.

Bella Winzar (8)
The Discovery School, West Malling

Space Hedgehog!

Space hedgehog, oh space hedgehog,
Are you soaring through the night?
You are flying out of sight,
Space hedgehog, oh space hedgehog,
Are you zooming fast?
And how long will your journey last?
Space hedgehog, oh space hedgehog,
Is it dark far from the sun?
Is being in space super fun?
Space hedgehog, oh space hedgehog,
Is it scary up in space?
Please come here, Earth is ace!
Space hedgehog, oh space hedgehog,
Do the aliens make you scream?
Wake up, it is just a dream!

Camille Prescott (7)
The Discovery School, West Malling

Fairyland

There once was a fairy called Poppy with wings that shimmered in the sun. She lived in a magical fairyland just behind my school. Whilst walking through the bluebell wood, that's where we met. With hair as black as the night sky, she flashed before my eyes.
She whispered her name and I told her mine. She showed me her home, such a tiny house! We laughed and played in those magical woods and made memories... I'll never forget!
Then I opened my eyes, and I was back in my bed. It felt so real, but was it just a dream?

Olivia Gorman (8)
The Discovery School, West Malling

The Football Game

Ode to the beautiful game,
Upon the fields of living green,
Where dreams and passions can be seen
A dance of joy and sweat begins
In the game of football, where all win,
From corner flags to centre spot,
Each player gives their very lot,
In unity, they play a part,
The ball of magic flight,
Waves thrown in the air with graceful might,
As players leap and twist and run,
Beneath the wonderful golden sun,
The crowd erupts in a wild applause.

Arhaan Pamnani (8)
The Discovery School, West Malling

The Dark Fairy!

There once was a dark and grim fairy,
With shiny black hair and bright green skin.
She would perk up at night,
Even if there was a fright.
She would always have a plan,
Even if a child was on land.
She was as naughty as a witch,
And she always loved a life's glitch.
She would also find a treat,
Even if she wasn't so neat.
This is the dark fairy
And she always has a plan!

Eden Lawson (8)
The Discovery School, West Malling

Fears Of The Night

F ears are scary
E very night
A lways freaky
R apid nights
S olo scares

O verwhelmed
F ear freakout

T ime is ticking until morning,
H owls of werewolves
E verything dark

N ot scared
I magination
G one wild again
H anging off the bed
T hinking of morning.

Max O'Brien (8)
The Discovery School, West Malling

World Cup Time

A big stadium was near.
But victory wasn't here.
Al Nassr Stadium was picked for the World Cup.
But they ran out of luck.
The score was 2-3.
Ronaldo scores and it's 3-3!
He is as scared as a fox.
Penalties are gonna start.
Three red cards were given before.
But that wasn't going to stop him score.
He won all, but not before
The end.

Rayaan Gul (8)
The Discovery School, West Malling

Dreamland

D on't worry about going to bed,
R ead yourself to sleep instead,
E very night we meet in a new place,
A lways a different and exciting new space,
M ore dreams, more places,
L ots of happy, smiling faces,
A land of cupcakes, love, wolves and treats,
N ever be scared to go to sleep,
D reamland is fun.

Lauren Lee (7)
The Discovery School, West Malling

Footballer Flying High

F lying high across the sky
O ne with summer night,
O n my way to play a match,
T his seemed to be a real delight,
B all so colourful,
A nd kits twinkling bright,
L egs kicking extra fast,
L egs freezing tight,
E xcited and happy to play...
R onaldo is on his way!

Andreas Hussain (7)
The Discovery School, West Malling

Rainbows And Marshmallow Clouds

When I go to sleep,
I dream of fluffy marshmallow clouds and bright, colourful rainbows.
Red, like the juiciest apples.
Orange, like the sunset at night.
Yellow, like the sourest lemon.
Green, like trees blowing in the wind.
Blue, like the sky.
Indigo, like the prettiest flowers, and
Violet, like my favourite slime.

Lucy Newton (8)
The Discovery School, West Malling

If I Had Superpowers

If I had superpowers, I would help the world.
If I had superpowers, I would take it away from those who don't deserve it.
If I had superpowers, I would give it to those who deserve it.
If I had superpowers, I would perk up others.
If I had superpowers, I would heal the world.

Monique Bailey (7)
The Discovery School, West Malling

Chocolate Cake

Chocolate cake, chocolate cake,
It will make my tummy ache.
After a while, the chocolate is gone.
No more chocolate, no more fun.
Oh, what's that?
It's chocolate,
I guess the chocolate feast can go back on!
But at the end, the chocolate has been eaten again.

Winston Wahlers (7)
The Discovery School, West Malling

Dream

D ream big dreams
R ainbow colours in our dreams
E xpressing my inner character in my dreams
A mazing adventures in our dreams
M ajestic thoughts in our dreams.

Flossie Wheatley (8)
The Discovery School, West Malling

YOUNG WRITERS INFORMATION

We hope you have enjoyed reading this book – and that you will continue to in the coming years.

If you're a young writer who enjoys reading and creative writing, or the parent of an enthusiastic poet or story writer, do visit our website **www.youngwriters.co.uk**. Here you will find free competitions, workshops and games, as well as recommended reads, a poetry glossary and our blog.

If you would like to order further copies of this book, or any of our other titles, then please give us a call or visit **www.youngwriters.co.uk**.

Young Writers
Remus House
Coltsfoot Drive
Peterborough
PE2 9BF
(01733) 890066
info@youngwriters.co.uk